CARVING FANTASY
CHARACTERS

CARVING FANTASY CHARACTERS

PATTERNS AND TECHNIQUES FOR 15 PROJECTS

Floyd Rhadigan

FOX CHAPEL
PUBLISHING

© 2012 by Floyd Rhadigan and Fox Chapel Publishing Company, Inc., East Petersburg, PA.

ISBN 978-1-56523-749-0

Library of Congress Cataloging-in-Publication Data

Rhadigan, Floyd.
 Carving fantasy characters / Floyd Rhadigan.
    p. cm.
 Includes index.
 ISBN 978-1-56523-749-0
 1. Wood-carved figurines. I. Title.
 TT199.7.R48 2012
 736'.4--dc23

To learn more about the other great books from Fox Chapel Publishing, or to find a retailer near you, call toll-free 800-457-9112 or visit us at *www.FoxChapelPublishing.com*.

Note to Authors: We are always looking for talented authors to write new books. Please send a brief letter describing your idea to Acquisition Editor, 1970 Broad Street, East Petersburg, PA 17520.

Printed in Indonesia
First printing

About the Author

Floyd Rhadigan was introduced to woodcarving by a family friend in 1970 and immediately took to it, carving as many projects as he could and eventually buying his first carving book in 1973. Due to a shortage of carving tools on the market, Rhadigan primarily completed his projects using a carving knife, until a book by Harold Enlow introduced him to palm tools. As Rhadigan's skills grew, he began developing his own carving style, which he describes as a mix between Ozark and Flat Plane Scandinavian styles. Rhadigan began teaching his carving techniques in 1976 for the Mt. Clemens Adult Education Program in Mt. Clemens, Michigan. He has also taught carving classes for Warren, Michigan's Parks and Recreation Department, and in Saline, Michigan. Rhadigan now teaches regularly for the Creative Woodcarving Seminar (Cadillac, Michigan) and the Michigan Woodcarvers Association (Oscoda, Michigan). In addition he gives annual classes at the Wood Carvers Roundup (Evart, Michigan) and the Northeast Wood Carvers Roundup (Honesdale, Pennsylvania) and conducts seminars for individuals and carving clubs. To learn more, visit *www.fantasycarving.com*.

Author Floyd Rhadigan.

Contents

Getting Started

I have always been a daydreamer. Thoughts of history and art blend together in my mind, helping me create a whimsical world of carvings. Whether you are new to carving or an old pro, the projects and patterns you'll find here will give you hours of carving enjoyment. I hope you have as much fun carving these projects as I had creating them. May we meet down the road sometime and sit down and carve.

Thank you for visiting my world!

— Floyd Rhadigan

Here are a handful of the tools I use when carving my fantasy creatures. You can use the ones listed on page 9 to carve your own projects, or you can select other tools that best suit you.

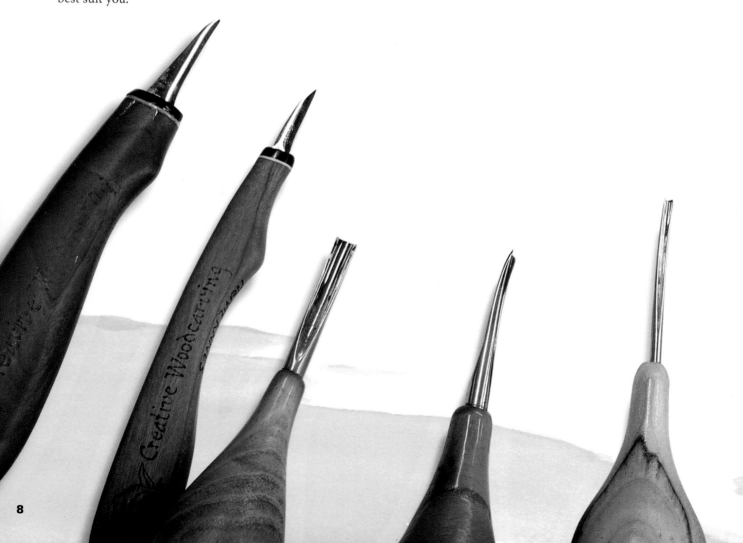

Basic Carving Instructions

I used a variety of palm tools to carve the projects in this booklet. Each project was made using the following tools:

- ½" (13mm) #9 gouge
- ½" (13mm) #7 gouge
- ½" (13mm) #3 gouge
- ¼" (6mm) #9 gouge
- ³⁄₁₆" (5mm) #9 gouge
- ⅛" (3mm) #9 gouge
- ¼" (6mm)-wide V-tool
- ³⁄₁₆" (5mm)-wide V-tool
- ⅛" (3mm)-wide V-tool
- 1¼" (32mm) bench knife
- ¾" (19mm) detail knife

You can use the tools I have listed or any other number of small gouges, V-tools, and knives you have on hand in your workshop and are comfortable using.

Keep your tools sharp by using a strop. You can also rub aluminum oxide stropping compound on a wood dowel or a length of wood shaped to the contour of your tools. By drawing the strop over the cutting edge, you can maintain sharp tools.

I prefer to use northern basswood for my carvings, because it carves well and will hold detail. All of the projects presented here were carved with the wood grain running up and down. To start carving your project, cut a wood blank to size and attach the front pattern. (If you'd like, you can purchase pre-cut blanks and rough outs from me by visiting *www.fantasycarving.com*, calling 734-649-3259, or by emailing me at *rhads134@comcast.net*.)

Cut the blank with a band saw, following the pattern. When I do this step, I leave a small tab of wood on the front of the cutout to help level the blank on the saw bed while I move on to cutting out the side view. Once you've cut out the front view, attach the side view pattern to your blank and cut it out with the saw.

Using the pictures of the project and pattern as a visual guide, start removing the excess wood from blank. Take your time; it is much easier to carve your piece to shape first and then carve in the details. Refer to your picture and pattern often.

I highly recommend wearing a Kevlar carving glove while you work. It is also important to keep your tools sharp. Sharp tools are actually much safer to work with than dull tools. Remember to take your time. Hasty work can result in a mistake on your carving or an accident with one of your tools.

Painting and Finishing

When your carving is all finished, make sure to sand away any remaining saw marks or other marks left on the wood as they accept paint and finish differently than carved areas. If left unsanded, these marks will be visible on the finished carving. Using a small scrub brush or denture brush, wash your carving with warm water and dish soap. Rinse it and let it dry.

Once your carving has dried, spray it with two light coats of a matte finish (I use Krylon #1311 Matte Finish). The finish will keep your paints from bleeding into each other as you work on your project. Always paint on your light colors first, and paint all background areas before adding the details.

Paint your projects using your preferred brand of acrylic paint. I use Jo Sonja and Delta Ceramcoat acrylic paints.

I prefer to thin the paint for my background colors, mixing twenty drops of water into every drop of paint. Diluting the paint this way allows the wood grain to show through the paint when the project is finished. For areas like the eyes, buttons, buckles, and other accessories like knives and swords, I don't thin the paint as much, allowing the color of these objects to stand out. If there is a specific part of your carving that you'd like to emphasize with color, paint it with a color you have only thinned a little bit. I also like to add flair to my carvings' clothing by adding pin stripes or a plaid pattern.

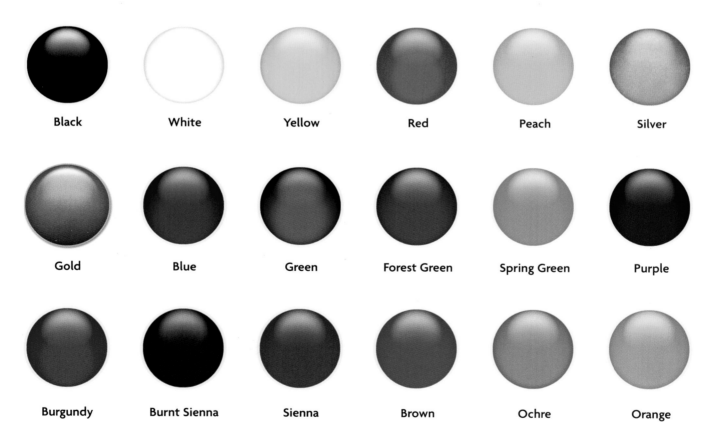

Black	White	Yellow	Red	Peach	Silver
Gold	Blue	Green	Forest Green	Spring Green	Purple
Burgundy	Burnt Sienna	Sienna	Brown	Ochre	Orange

Color chart. These are some of the various colors I use for my carvings. I choose to use Jo Sonja and Delta Ceramcoat acrylic paints, but you can use your preferred brand of acrylic paint and vary the color choices as you desire.

Painting the eyes

I think the eyes bring life to any carving. The steps below demonstrate the method I use to paint eyes on my carvings and bring them to life. Before you start, cover the entire eye and eyelid area of your carving with a layer of flesh-colored paint and let dry.

Once you have finished painting, spray on one more coat of matte finish. Then, use a finishing wax to antique your carving. I use Watco Satin Finish Wax, making a mixture of about 70 percent natural wax and 30 percent dark wax. Use a small, stiff bristled brush to apply the wax to the entire carving. Pat it dry with a paper towel or rag to remove any excess, and then buff the carving.

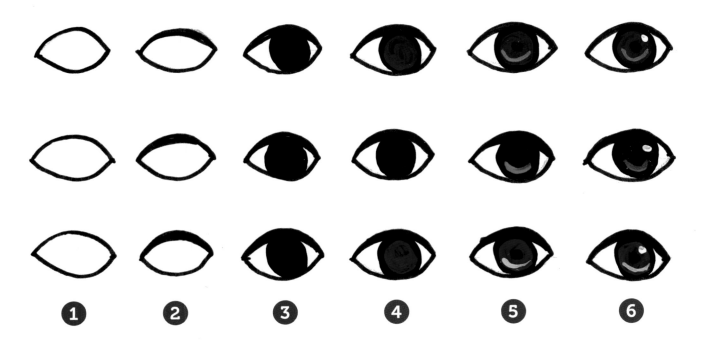

Painting Steps

1. Thin white paint just a bit and paint the eyeball, trying not to hit the lids. Let the paint dry*.
2. Use black to paint along the edge of the upper eyelid to thicken the lid.
3. Paint on the iris using black paint. I prefer to put the iris closer to the inner or outer corner of the eye. I find that placing the iris directly in the middle of the eye gives the carving a straight, blank stare. Let the paint dry.
4. Paint the iris color (blue, brown, or green) inside the black iris circle you painted during Step 3. Paint the colored circle small enough that a black ring surrounds the colored paint when you are finished.
5. Paint a small crescent on the lower part of the iris, using light blue on blues eyes, orange on brown eyes, and light green on green eyes. Then, use black to paint the pupil in the center of the iris.
6. Paint a speck of white on one side of the upper iris.

Note that you can use a hair dryer to help dry the paint and speed this process along.

Tork the Troll

This sinister fellow invites you in with a welcoming candle, but his big smile hides his true intent.

Start by roughing out the front and side profiles of the carving with a band saw. Mark the major areas where you need to eliminate wood. On the front of the blank, you need to remove the excess wood beside the arm holding the candle. On the back of the blank, remove the excess wood beside the arm holding the knife. Mark the location of the troll's right elbow so you don't remove too much wood from the back.

Materials:

- A basswood blank cut to 6½" (165mm) high, 3" wide (76mm), and 2½" (64mm) deep
- Dish soap
- Krylon matte finish
- Watco natural finishing wax
- Watco dark finishing wax
- Paper towels
- Jo Sonja acrylic paints: Medium Flesh, Cadmium Orange, White, Burgundy, Moss Green, Dark Gray, Yellow, Burnt Sienna, Metallic Gold, Yellow Base, Red, Metallic Silver, Black, and Pthalo Blue

Tools:

- Carving knife
- Detail knife
- #3 gouge: ½" (13mm)
- #7 gouge: ⅜" (10mm)
- #9 gouge: ¼" (6mm), 3⁄16" (5mm)
- 45° V-tools: ¼" (6mm), 3⁄16" (5mm), ⅛" (3mm)
- Micro gouges: 5⁄32" (4mm), ⅛" (3mm)
- Scrub brush
- Paintbrushes
- Pencil

Special Sources: *Basswood rough outs of Tork the Troll are available for $18 plus s&h. Contact Floyd Rhadigan at 734-649-3259 or visit www.fantasycarving.com.*

The author used these products for the project. Substitute your choice of brands, tools, and materials as desired.

Rough out the character

Rough out the knife-holding arm. Sketch in the arm, and use a knife to make a stop cut along the lines. Carve up to the stop cut with a ½" (13mm) #3 gouge. Draw the top of the shoulder, and carve along the line with a ¼" (6mm) 45° V-tool. Then, remove the waste with a ½" (13mm) #3 gouge or a knife. Thin the back and side of the arm.

Rough out the candle-holding arm. Draw in the candle-holding arm. Make sure the tops of both shoulders are the same height. Draw in the elbow, and use a ¼" (6mm) 45° V-tool to isolate the shoulder. Use a knife to shape and thin the shoulder. Then, use a knife to thin the wrist and remove wood from under the candle-holding hand.

Rough out the head. Draw a centerline down the front of the head and down each side of the head. Use a knife to round the head in toward the area where the nose sticks out. Remove the sharp corners from the back of the head and shave away the excess wood from in front of the ears. Draw in the bandanna knot.

Rough out the bandanna. Carve around the knot with a ¼" (6mm) 45° V-tool to separate the knot from the rest of the bandanna. Carve away the excess wood with a knife. Make a stop cut in the center of the tails and around the outside of the tails, and carve up to the stop cuts with a knife to remove the waste. Draw in the bandanna where it comes down from the top of the ear diagonally to cover most of the right eye. Continue the line to the back, and carve along the line with a ¼" (6mm) 45° V-tool. Thin the back of the ear with a knife, and then carve up to the V-tool cut to separate the bandanna from the forehead and the hair.

Rough in the nose and eyes. Use a ¼" (6mm) #9 gouge to thin the nose. The nose should be about ¼" (6mm) from the centerline on both sides. Use a knife to round and shape the nose. Use the ¼" (6mm) #9 gouge to shape the top of the nose where it meets the brow to create a nice transition from the face to the bridge of the nose. Remove the high spots from the face using a knife. Draw a semicircle at the top of the eyes. Remove some wood from inside the pencil lines with a ¼" (6mm) #9 gouge. Use a knife to remove some wood under the bandanna to indicate the covered eye.

Rough in the nose and cheeks. Use a ³⁄₁₆" (5mm) #9 gouge to carve up along both sides of the nose. The goal is to make the bridge of the nose stand out from the cheeks and eye area. Deepen the cuts near the bridge of the nose on the fully exposed eye. Carve up alongside the nose, and then carve from the outside edge of the eye socket in toward the bridge of the nose. Round the cheeks with a knife. Draw the sideburn and the hair hanging down behind the ear. Make a stop cut along the lines with a detail knife and carve up to the stop cuts to separate the sideburns.

Rough out the hair. Thin the ear with a knife. Make a stop cut along the bottom of the ear and along the side of the hair hanging behind the ear. Carve up to the stop cuts to separate the ear and jaw from the hair. Thin the area under the jaw and shape the front of the neck. Make a stop cut along the hairline and cut up to the stop cut to isolate the hairline between the bandanna ties. Shape the face and under the jaw.

Carve the face

Shape the sides of the nose. Position a ⅜" (10mm) #7 gouge upside down on the tip of the nose and carve from the tip down to the cheek to shape the outer flange of the nostrils. Use a detail knife to clean up any roughness on top of the nose. Continue the cut around the nostril flange and up around to the top of the nose with a detail knife. Carve up to this cut to remove a wedge of wood. The top of the wedge marks the start of the cheek. Draw the cheek and use a detail knife to stop cut along the line. Carve up to the stop cut to create the upper lip and cheek. Carve deep lines to create depth and shadows. Use the knife to start forming the mouth barrel and to carve away some of the excess wood around the candle so you can carve the right side of the troll's mouth.

tip

Carving the candle separately
You can carve the candle separately and glue it onto the carving. If you're looking for a challenge, carve the entire piece from a single block of wood.

Carve the mouth. Draw the bottom lip line up into the corners of the cheek line to create a big grin. Carve along the line with a ³⁄₁₆" (5mm) 45° V-tool. Deepen the cut with a carving knife, and use the knife to shape the chin area before you draw in the fangs. Stop cut along the fangs with a detail knife, and carve up to the stop cuts to separate the fangs from the lip and chin area.

Carve the eyes. Draw in a lateral line to separate the top and bottom of the eye. Draw in the upper and lower lids. Cut along the upper lid with a detail knife, making the cut deeper in the corners. Round the eye up to the upper lid. Stop cut along the lower lid, again cutting deeper in the corners. Round the rest of the eye down to the lower lid to create a round eyeball. Use a ⅛" (3mm) 45° V-tool to carve the shadow between the upper eyelid and the brow. Then, carve the lower eyelid using the same technique. Make the lower eyelid a little puffy, and tuck the lower lid under the upper eyelid in the corner. Use the V-tool to add crow's feet.

Carve the nostrils. Use a ⅜" (10mm) #7 gouge to remove the saw marks and fuzz from the neck. Then, use a ⁵⁄₃₂" (4mm) micro gouge to carve the nostrils. Push the gouge straight in the whole way to the upper lip to carve the nostril opening. Do not try to pry the chip free; use a detail knife to free the chip and refine the upper lip.

Carve the hair. Use a knife to round the hair up to the bandanna. Smooth the hair before you carve the texture. Carve a series of grooves with a ³⁄₁₆" (5mm) #9 gouge. Carve up toward the bandanna and down toward the back. Use a knife to free the chips. Carve between the gouge marks with a ⅛" (3mm) 45° V-tool using the same technique. Free the chips with a knife, and use the knife to undercut the bandanna slightly to separate it from the hair.

Carve the ears. Scoop out the inside of the ear with a ³⁄₈" (10mm) #7 gouge. Draw in the tragus and use a ⁵⁄₃₂" (4mm) micro gouge to make a stop cut along the tragus and along the line from the tragus to the top of the ear. Carve up to the stop cut with a detail knife to hollow the ear.

Add the details

Refine the bandanna. Draw in the bandanna folds—all of the folds flow toward the knot. Carve flowing grooves with a ½" (13mm) #9 gouge to give the bandanna some movement. Use a ³⁄₁₆" (5mm) 45° V-tool to carve a few creases in the bandanna. Carve a crease in the knot and in the tails with a ³⁄₁₆" (5mm) #9 gouge. Deepen the gouge lines in the tails with a ⅛" (3mm) 45° V-tool.

Carve the candle-holding arm. Draw a line from the armpit to the elbow on the back of the arm holding the candle. Make a stop cut on the line and carve to the stop cut from both sides to round the arm and round the back. Use a knife to carve the crease where the arm is bent at the elbow. Draw lines to show where the sleeve ends, and make a line ¼" (6mm) back from the end of the sleeve for the cuff. Carve along the end of the sleeve with a ¼" (6mm) 45° V-tool. Then, carve along the cuff line. Taper the cuff so it's skinnier where it meets the shirt than it is where it meets the wrist to block out the form. This will allow you to carve ruffles later.

Carve the hand. Thin the hand back toward the cuff. Draw in the thumb and outline of the fingers, and make shallow cuts along the lines with a ³⁄₁₆" (5mm) 45° V-tool. Make stop cuts in the V-tool grooves, and carve away the excess wood between the thumb and fingers. Shape the planes of the hand, keeping it somewhat flat across the knuckles. Remember, the palm is extended and the fingers are turned up. Use a ¼" (6mm) 45° V-tool to carve a line across the top of the fingertips.

Hand proportions

tip

For most hands, the distance from the base of the fingers to the first knuckle is half the length of the thumb. It's about half that distance from the first knuckle to the second knuckle. Likewise, the distance from the second knuckle to the tip of the finger is half the distance between the first and second knuckles.

Separate the fingers. Draw a centerline down the planes of the fingers. Split the two areas on either side of the centerline in half to form four fingers. Carve along the lines with a ³⁄₁₆" (5mm) #9 gouge. Carve individual lines along each of the planes. Use a knife to make football-shaped cuts between the fingers. The fingers are thin between the knuckles and thick at the knuckles. Draw in the other side of the hand, stop cut along the line, and carve up to the stop cut to separate the candle from the hand.

Carve the candle. The candle sits on top of a tray with the tops of the fingers even with the base of the candle. Make a stop cut on either side of the tray's handle—use a 2" (51mm)-long knife to get behind the handle next to the body. Be careful not to cut the nose off. Clean up the back of the handle with a ³⁄₁₆" (5mm) #9 gouge. Finish shaping the handle, and then drill the hole in the handle with a small bit or a small micro gouge. Carve grooves between the fingertips. Make a stop cut around the base of the candle and thin the candle down to the stop cut. Use a detail knife to carve the flame. Clean up the chest with a knife and remove any fuzz.

Shape the knife-holding arm. Draw in the shape of the arm and carve the crease above the arm where the arm bends behind the back with a ¼" (6mm) #9 gouge. Thin the arm and carve the armpit. Then, carve the cuff and end of the sleeve the same way you carved the other sleeve. Use a ³⁄₁₆" (5mm) 45° V-tool to carve the top of the thumb and hand. Then, carve around the bottom of the thumb and cut in the puffy palm before dropping down to the hilt of the knife. Carve two parallel lines to represent the hilt. Use a detail knife to make a stop cut in the V-grooves and remove the waste between the palm and the hilt and remove the excess wood below the hilt.

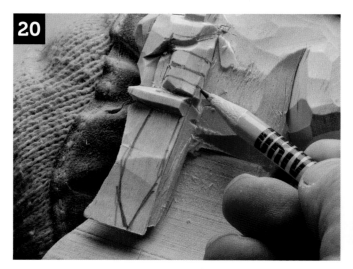

Finish carving the knife. Draw in the fingers holding the hilt. You should see a bit of the handle. Draw in the shape of the blade. Carve between the fingers with a ³⁄₁₆" (5mm) #9 gouge, and then make the football-shaped cuts between the fingers with a detail knife. Shape the blade of the knife. Thin the blade, mainly from the side of the blade closest to the back. Do not remove too much wood from the outside of the blade. Remove the fuzz from the back with a knife, and flatten the back and torso to remove a bit of the roundness.

Carve the feet. Draw the shape of the feet onto the bottom and remove the excess wood with a knife. Cut toward your thumb to maintain control. Then, carve out a wedge of wood between the feet in the toe and heel area. Use a knife to carve the toes so they turn upward. Draw in the shape of the shoes and carve along the lines with a ³⁄₁₆" (5mm) 45° V-tool to separate the shoes from the pants. Make a stop cut inside the V-grooves with a knife.

Shape the belly, buttocks, and legs. Draw a line to separate the belly from the legs. Carve under the line around the belly with a ¼" (6mm) 45° V-tool. Use a knife to round the belly and buttocks, relieving the legs as you work the belly. Generally, male buttocks are square and female buttocks are pear-shaped. Use a knife to make a stop cut between the legs in the front and remove a wedge of wood to separate the legs. Refine the separation of the legs in the back and clean up the legs and belly.

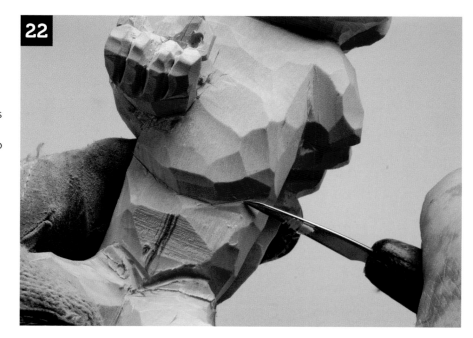

Add the final details

Carve the shirt and vest. Pencil in the open collar of the shirt and vest. Make a stop cut along the bottom of the collar with a detail knife, and use a long-bladed knife to carve up to the stop cut to separate the collar from the shirt. Use the detail knife to make a stop cut around the vest. Carve up to the stop cut to separate the vest from the shirt. Use a long-bladed knife in the area behind the candle.

Finish the shoes. Carve just under the top of the shoes with a ¼" (6mm) #9 gouge to create a collar or lip along the top of the shoes. Use a ³⁄₁₆" (5mm) #9 gouge to carve wrinkles in the top of the shoes, the crotch, behind the knees, and in the crooks of the arms. Deepen the wrinkles with a ³⁄₁₆" (5mm) 45° V-tool. Carve away the sharp edge from the sole around the bottom of the foot. Remove wood from below the toes to create the point on the toes.

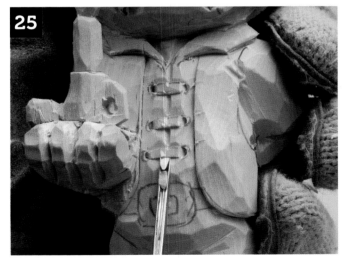

Add the shirt and belt details. Draw in the shirt ties and buckle. Make eyelet holes at each end of ties on both sides of the shirt using a ⅛" (3mm) micro gouge. Create a half circle at the end of each tie and use a detail knife to connect the lace from eyelet to eyelet. Carve away the wood from the shirt around the laces to make the laces stand out. Carve the shirt line between the ties with a ⅛" (3mm) V-tool. Make a stop cut around the belt buckle with a detail knife, and carve up to the buckle so it stands out. Then, make a stop cut on the inside of the buckle, and carve away the wood inside the buckle. Cut in the little bit of belt that is showing using a detail knife.

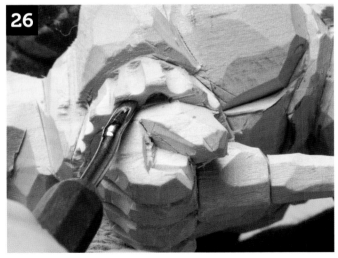

Carve the ruffles. Use a ³⁄₁₆" (5mm) #9 gouge to carve a groove from the hand toward the sleeve. Leave a space the same width as the gouge, and then carve another groove. Use a micro gouge to undercut the high areas on the ruffles. Free the chips with a carving knife. Then, carve the trim on the vest with a ⅛" (3mm) V-tool. Go over the carving and remove any remaining saw marks or fuzz.

Painting the Troll

Scrub the carving with dish soap, hot water, and a scrub brush to remove any pencil marks or grease. Allow it to dry and apply two light coats of Krylon matte spray finish.

For most of the paint colors, I thin one drop of acrylic paint with twenty drops of water to create thin washes of color. For the hands and face, use Medium Flesh. For the hair, use Cadmium Orange. The shirt is White, and the bandanna is Burgundy. Use Moss Green for the pants and Dark Gray for the inside of the vest. The trim on the vest and the shirt laces are Yellow. Use Burnt Sienna for the boots and knife handle and Metallic Gold for the candlestick, belt buckle, design on the vest, and knife hilt. Use slightly thinned White for the candle and fangs, and Yellow Base for the flame. Add a little Red to the tip of the flame, and use Metallic Sliver for the knife blade. Use highly thinned Red to add a blush to the tip of the ear, top of the nostrils, and the lower lip.

To paint the eyes, give the eyeballs a White base coat, and allow the paint to dry. Then, paint the entire iris on each eye Black, and allow the paint to dry. Add a little White to Pthalo Blue, paint the irises, and allow the paint to dry. Add a little more White to make a pale blue and add a small crescent on the bottom of the colored part of the iris. Paint in the Black pupil in the center of the iris, and when the Black is dry, add a tiny spot of White in the upper part of the pupil.

After the paint is dry, seal the carving with another coat of Krylon matte spray finish. Create a mixture of 70 percent Watco dark finishing wax mixed with 30 percent Watco natural finishing wax and apply the mixture to the carving with a brush. Allow it to sit for a minute and then wipe off the wax with a paper towel. Buff the carving with a clean paper towel. Dispose of the paper towels carefully; as the wax contains boiled linseed oil, the paper towels can spontaneously combust.

The Trolls of Legend

Trolls are rascally characters referenced throughout Norse mythology and Scandinavian folklore. For the most part, they are described as troublemakers who disturb and annoy humans, but are not malicious.

Most trolls lived isolated from human society in dark places like mountains, under rocks, and in caves. They did not like sunlight, and in fact, some legends state that trolls exposed to sunlight turned into stone. Many trolls are described as ugly and grotesque dim-witted creatures, while others are said to have a human appearance and are set apart only by their lack of Christian faith.

Trolls often claimed ownership of lakes, forests, and bridges, something that put them in conflict with humans who made similar claims. Some trolls might have demanded payment from travelers or threatened anyone trying to pass through their territory, as in the story "Three Billy Goats Gruff." They enjoyed playing tricks on humans, walking up behind them and kicking them, or making them slip on logs in the forest. Trolls would sometimes try to destroy churches by throwing rocks at them, perhaps because they were frightened by the church bells. Mountain trolls, the largest trolls, could cause destructive earthquakes and avalanches by stomping their feet. In many cases, specific trolls were associated with undesirable human traits or sins. There were some benevolent trolls, however. These typically lived on human farms and helped care for the animals.

Front

Left

Back

Right

Tork the Troll

FRONT

LEFT

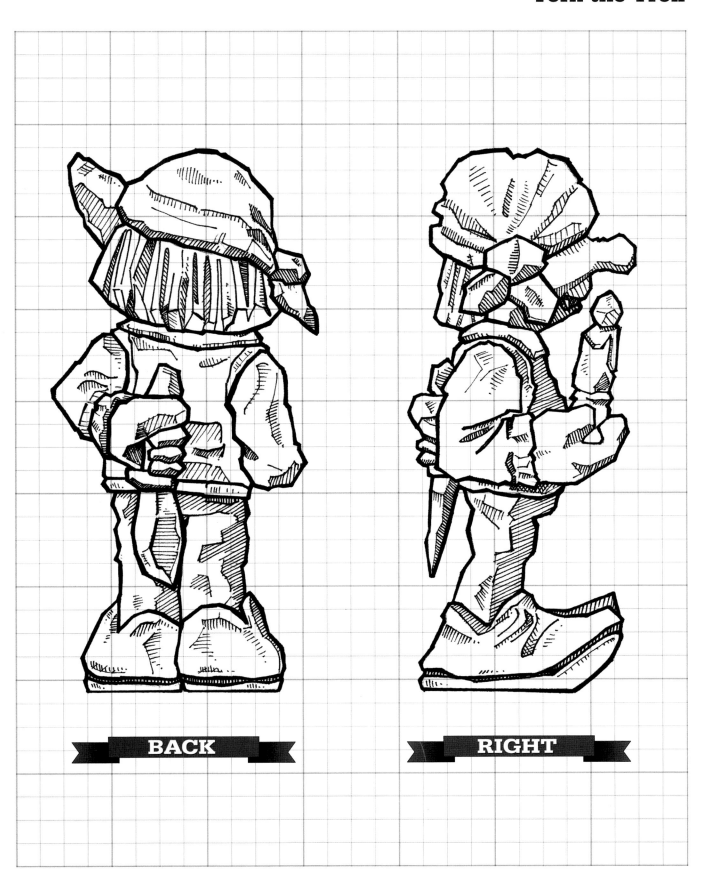

BACK

RIGHT

Olga

Olga is a proud Viking woman who is happiest when she's paired with Erik the Red (see page 30).

Materials:

- A blank cut to 5" (127mm) high, 2¼" (57mm) wide, and 2¼" (57mm) deep
- Krylon matte finish
- Watco natural finishing wax
- Watco dark finishing wax
- Acrylic paints of choice (I use Black, White, Flesh, Blue, Purple, Olive Green, and Raw Sienna by Jo Sonja and Delta Ceramcoat)

Tools:

- Carving knives, gouges, and V-tools of choice
- Band saw
- Pencil

Special Sources: *Basswood rough outs of Olga are available for $15 plus s&h. Contact Floyd Rhadigan at 734-649-3259 or visit www.fantasycarving.com.*

The author used these products for the project. Substitute your choice of brands, tools, and materials as desired.

| Front | Left | Back | Right |

Olga: Princess and Saint

Olga is a 900s historical figure of Russia whose life is documented in numerous historical records, one of the most trusted being the Russian Primary Chronicle. Olga's deeds are also described in legendary tales, the historical validity of which is questioned by some of today's historians. It is thought Olga was born in Pskov and that she was of Scandinavian origin, possibly a descendant of Varyags, or Vikings. In the beginning of the 900s, Olga married Prince Igor, Prince of Novgorod and ruler of Kiev, or Kievan Rus. Igor was the son of Rurik, said to be the founder of Russia.

In the 940s, Igor was murdered by members of the Drevlyans, a Slavic tribe he had visited to collect tributes to Kiev. As Igor's son, Svyatoslav, was only three at the time of his father's death, Olga became ruler of Kiev with the full support of the Rus army. She exacted revenge against the Drevlyans, killing members of the tribe and burning one of their towns.

When Svyatoslav came of age, he spent much of his rule travelling with the army, executing military campaigns to grow Kiev. While her son was away, Olga continued to manage the affairs of the state. She is considered an intelligent and strong ruler, creating a policy of tribute payment to the state (perhaps the first instance of legal taxation in Eastern Europe), building cities to act as trade centers, and organizing Kiev into regions to be managed by individuals she appointed.

One of Olga's most notable acts was her conversion to Christianity. It is thought she was baptized in Constantinople in the 950s. Although Olga was in contact with church officials in both the Byzantine and Roman empires, she chose to worship following the Byzantine tradition, which would later form the Greek Orthodox Church.

Olga died circa 970 and was buried according to Christian tradition at Svyatoslav's request. The Orthodox Church declared her a saint in 1547.

Olga

FRONT

LEFT

BACK

RIGHT

Erik the Red

From the horns on his helmet to the blade of his ax, you'll enjoy carving this friendly Viking. Match him with Olga (page 26) to make a perfect pair.

Materials:

- A blank cut to 5½" (140mm) high, 2¾" (70mm) wide, and 2⅜" (60mm) deep
- Krylon matte finish
- Watco natural finishing wax
- Watco dark finishing wax
- Acrylic paints of choice (I use Black, White, Raw Sienna, Flesh, Olive Green, Burnt Sienna, Orange, Silver, Bronze, and Blue by Jo Sonja and Delta Ceramcoat)

Tools:

- Carving knives, gouges, and V-tools of choice
- Band saw
- Pencil

Special Sources: *Basswood rough outs of Erik the Red are available for $15 plus s&h. Contact Floyd Rhadigan at 734-649-3259 or visit www.fantasycarving.com.*

The author used these products for the project. Substitute your choice of brands, tools, and materials as desired.

Front

Left

Back

Right

Erik the Red: A Viking Explorer

The life of Erik the Red is recounted in sagas of Icelandic origin. Although he was born in Norway, Erik spent most of his early life in Iceland after his father was exiled from Norway for killing a man. In Iceland, Erik married Thorhild, but after a dispute with his neighbor and an argument with a friend over religious artifacts that resulted in the deaths of two men, Erik was banned from Iceland for three years. Erik decided to spend his time in exile exploring islands that were to the west of Iceland, including present-day Greenland.

Although Erik is often credited with discovering Greenland, Gunnbjörn Ulfsson was actually the first person to report sighting the island and Snaebjörn Galti attempted to form a settlement on the island around 970. Erik spent his three years away from Iceland sailing around and exploring the southern tip of Greenland. At the end of his banishment, he returned to Iceland to bring settlers to the island, convinced it was a better location for farming than Iceland. Settling in a new location would also allow Erik to separate himself from those in Iceland who were displeased with him. Erik sailed for Greenland with twenty-some ships, arriving with about fourteen, and between 300 and 500 settlers.

Erik had four children: three sons and two daughters. His son Leif Eriksson is credited as the first European to arrive on the shores of North America. Although not during his lifetime, Erik's Greenland settlement eventually died out, most likely because of harsh conditions, disease, or Inuit attacks. Other Norse settlements on the island were successful, however.

Two Vikings, Olga and Erik make a perfect pair. Carve them both and place them together in your home. They can decorate a table or watch over both ends of your fireplace mantle.

Erik the Red

FRONT

LEFT

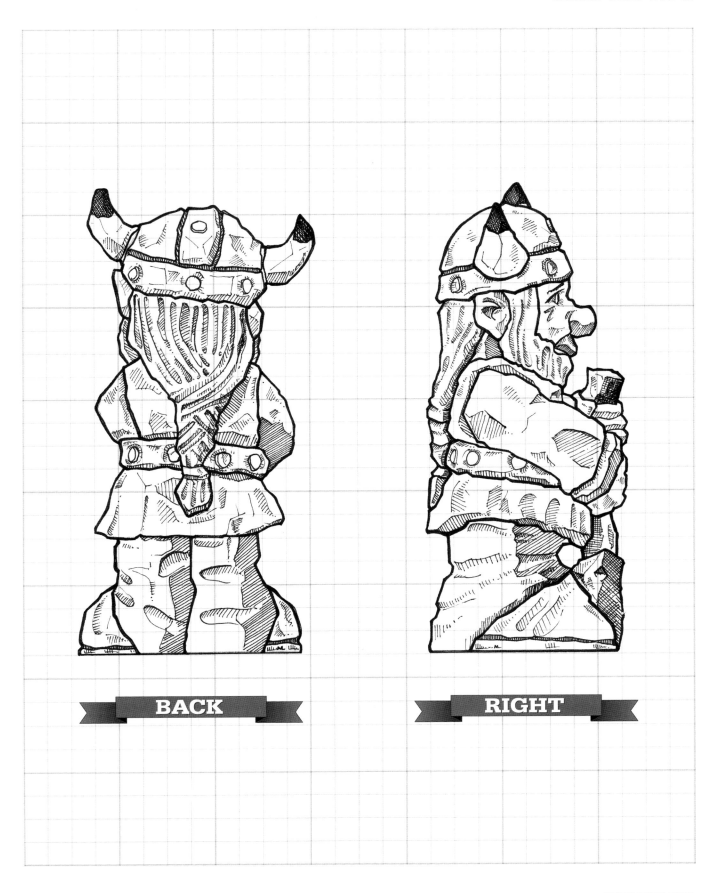

BACK

RIGHT

Merlin

This carving is my interpretation of the famous wizard from King Arthur's court. You're sure to feel his magic as you bring him to life.

Materials:

- A blank cut to 6" (152mm) high, 2½" (64mm) wide, and 2" (51mm) deep
- Krylon matte finish
- Watco natural finishing wax
- Watco dark finishing wax
- Acrylic paints of choice (I use White, Flesh, Burgundy, Gold, Black, Blue, and Yellow by Jo Sonja and Delta Ceramcoat)

Tools:

- Carving knives, gouges, and V-tools of choice
- Band saw
- Pencil

Special Sources: *Basswood rough outs of Merlin are available for $15 plus s&h. Contact Floyd Rhadigan at 734-649-3259 or visit www.fantasycarving.com.*

The author used these products for the project. Substitute your choice of brands, tools, and materials as desired.

| Front | Left | Back | Right |

Merlin: Fact or Fiction?

The wizard Merlin is a character found in the Arthurian Romances, a collection of stories written during the Middle Ages that describes the history of Britain in the fifth century after the end of Roman power in the region. According to the romances, Merlin was a mystic bard who was responsible for saving the kingdom by contriving to make Arthur the king. He then served as Arthur's advisor, helping establish the Round Table and arranging for the Lady of the Lake to give the sword Excalibur to Arthur. He was the protector of the Holy Grail and helped reunite Arthur's knights when they fell into disagreement after Arthur became ill.

Although most maintain Merlin is a fictional character, there is evidence to suggest the character "Merlin" of the Arthurian Romances was based on the historical figure Ambrosius Aurelius. Ambrosius is a figure appearing in multiple historical texts from the Dark Ages. He is said to have united Britain during the fifth century by leading the British army to victory against the invading Saxons.

The connection between Merlin and Ambrosius comes from two separate texts, one written during the 800s and the other during the 1100s that discuss a story surrounding the British ruler Vortigern. Both tell the tale of a boy who used "mystic" powers to save himself from being sacrificed by Vortigern and as a result became revered by the king. The older text names the boy as Ambrosius, while the more recent names him as Merlin. Outside the different names, the stories are almost identical. Evidence suggests the 1100s text used the name "Merlin" because it was a title Ambrosius had taken, meaning "the Eagle." At the time, it was common for British soldiers to adopt animal battle names. In fact, it has been suggested that Arthur was actually a title meaning "bear." Whether he is a purely fictional character or a historical figure, Merlin is sure to continue to inspire us in the modern world.

Merlin

FRONT

LEFT

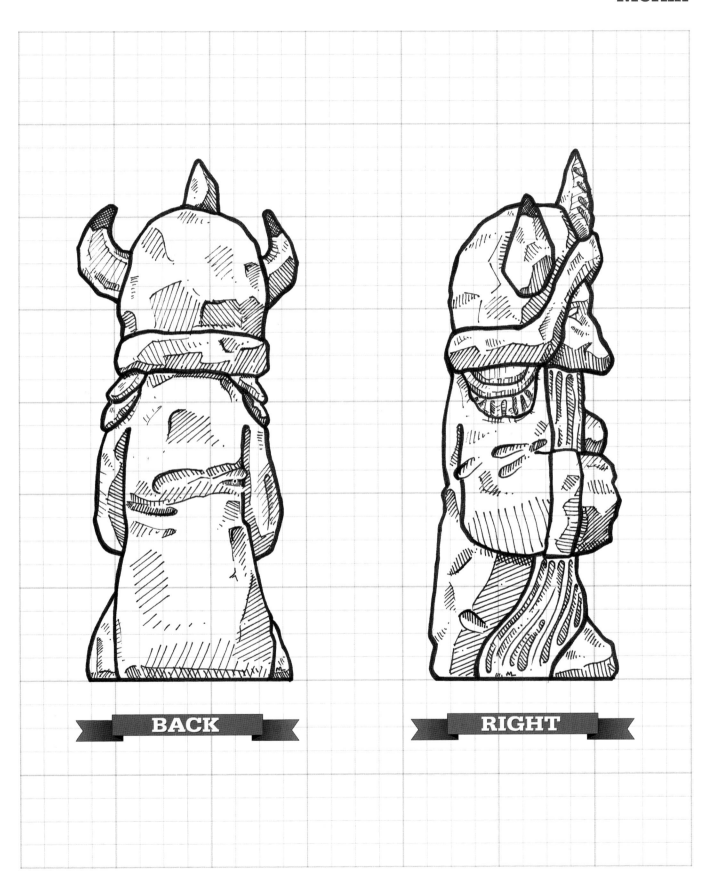

BACK

RIGHT

Cortney

Cortney is a sweet, young elf, ready to lounge on your shelf. Before you start carving, do some research on the anatomy of human hands and feet or study some pictures. This will help make your carving's features more realistic.

Materials:

- A blank cut to
  5⅝" (143mm) high,
  2¼" (57mm) wide, and
  3⅝" (92mm) deep
- Krylon matte finish
- Watco natural
  finishing wax
- Watco dark finishing wax
- Acrylic paints of choice
  (I use Flesh, Orange,
  Burgundy, Red, Blue,
  Black, and White
  by Jo Sonja and
  Delta Ceramcoat)

Tools:

- Carving knives, gouges, and V-tools of choice
- Band saw
- Pencil

Special Sources: *Basswood rough outs of Cortney are available for $16 plus s&h. Contact Floyd Rhadigan at 734-649-3259 or visit www.fantasycarving.com.*

The author used these products for the project. Substitute your choice of brands, tools, and materials as desired.

Front

Left

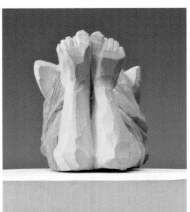

Back

The Elves of Mythology

You can find hundreds of varied descriptions of elves across many cultures, from supernatural, immortal beings and mischievous pranksters, to diminutive toymakers and members of a separate race. In German mythology, the word for elf was originally used to indicate any kind of spirit or supernatural being. Later, however, it specifically referenced one type of creature, usually of small size and with a human appearance. These elves were divided into two groups: light and dark. This distinction was a matter of coloring rather than an indication of a good or evil nature. Light elves had fair features, while dark elves had dark skin and glowing eyes.

Elves were held responsible for the unfortunate events that impacted the lives of humans, such as injury to livestock and disease. *Alpdrücken*, the German word for nightmare, translated literally as "elf-pressure," can be traced back to the belief that elves would sit on a sleeping person's chest and give them bad dreams. Elves were also thought to steal human children and replace them with changelings.

Elves are depicted differently in other cultures, often referenced as benevolent beings that would aid humans or as members of a separate race who entered human society seeking love. The elves depicted in J. R. R. Tolkien's *The Lord of the Rings* series certainly mimic some of these qualities of legend, from their kindness and longevity, to their superhuman capabilities.

Right

Cortney

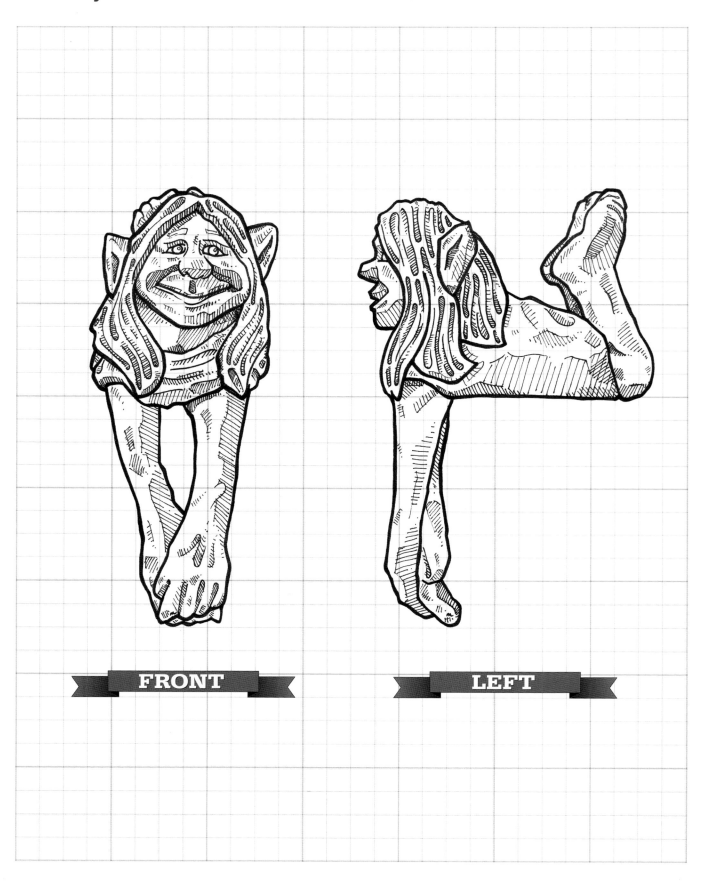

FRONT

LEFT

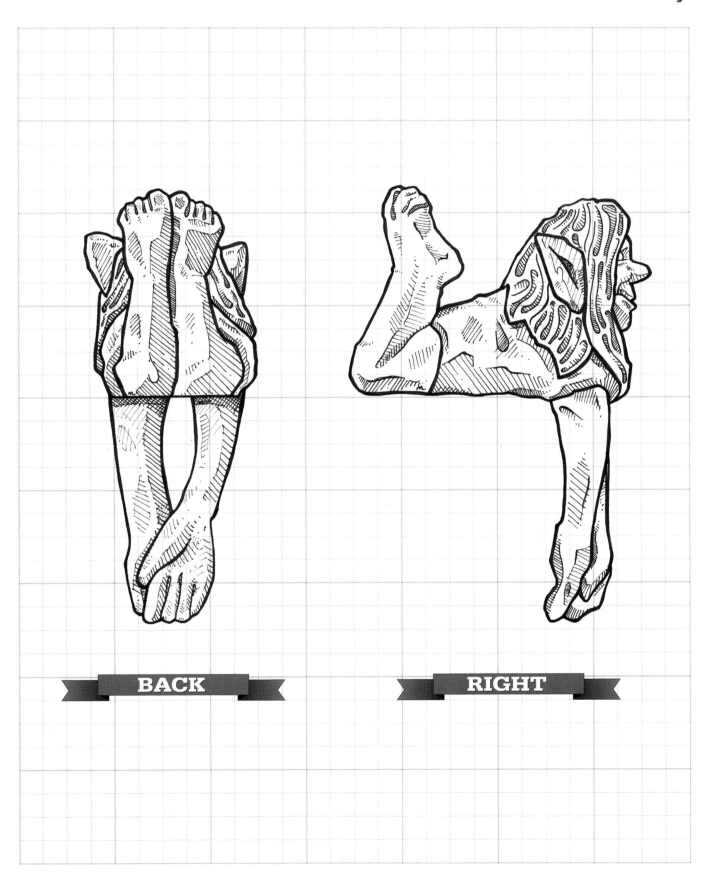

BACK

RIGHT

Nicole the Pixie

Nicole adorns any shelf with just a little bit of magic. To make carving the details of her raised arm and crossed leg easier, use a drill with a small bit to make a hole at the crook of her arm and in the space between her crossed legs. The holes will make it easier to work in these areas with your carving tools.

Materials:

- A blank cut to 6" (152mm) high, 3" (76mm) wide, and 3" (76mm) deep
- Krylon matte finish
- Watco natural finishing wax
- Watco dark finishing wax
- Acrylic paints of choice (I use Flesh, Hookers Green, Burgundy, Blue, Black, and White by Jo Sonja and Delta Ceramcoat)

Tools:

- Carving knives, gouges, and V-tools of choice
- Band saw
- Pencil

Special Sources: *Basswood rough outs of Nicole the Pixie are available for $16 plus s&h. Contact Floyd Rhadigan at 734-649-3259 or visit www.fantasycarving.com.*

The author used these products for the project. Substitute your choice of brands, tools, and materials as desired.

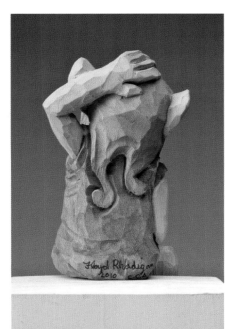

Front   **Left**   **Back**

A Brief History of Pixies

Although the words fairy, pixie, and elf are often used interchangeably, all three are distinct beings that appear in the myths and legends of cultures around the world. Pixies refer to beings that appear primarily in British mythology, and the word pixie is generally accepted as being Celtic in origin. Pixies are primarily found in the south of England, particularly in Devon, Somerset, and Cornwall. Although modern depictions often show pixies with wings, it is not clear whether this was part of the original pixie legend. Pixies are thought to be small, often described as no larger than the human hand; however, some tales suggest pixies could vary their size and, therefore, appear larger if they chose. Pixies are typically described as poorly clothed or without clothes altogether and incredibly beautiful.

Some stories claim pixies were kind creatures that would aid humans of whom they were fond. Other tales depict pixies as tricksters, particularly known for stealing human possessions, harassing kitchen maids, stealing horses to go on night rides, or kidnapping children. A pixie's favorite trick, however, was leading travellers astray. In fact, humans could be so affected by the pixie that they would wander through the countryside, unaware of their surroundings, singing or speaking in tongues. This condition was known as being "pixie-led," which has a correlation to the modern word "pixilated," meaning mentally unbalanced or bemused.

Right

Nicole the Pixie

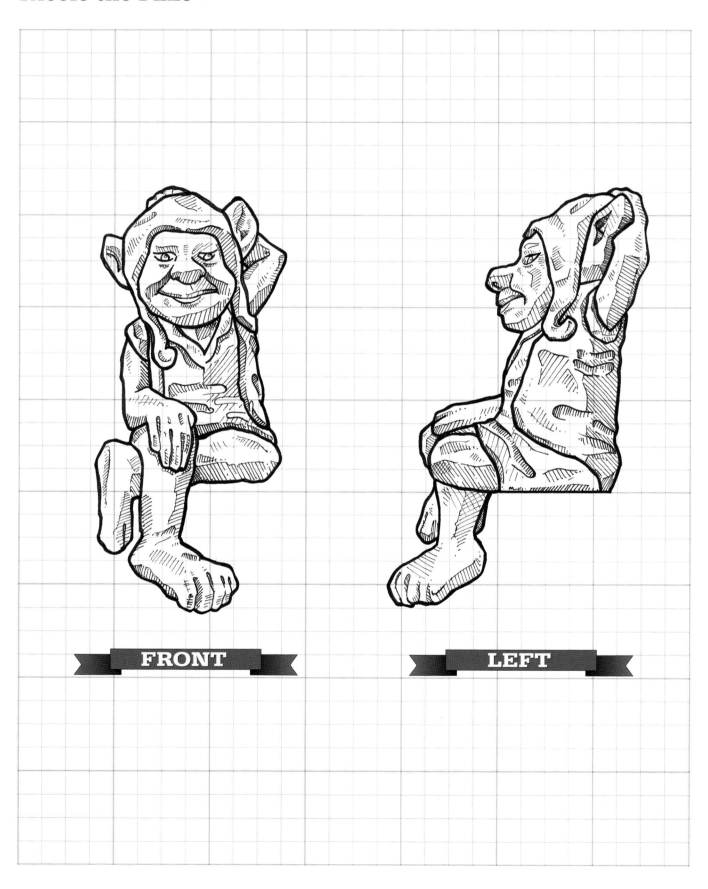

FRONT

LEFT

BACK

RIGHT

A Gnome with a View

In my mind, mushrooms have a place in the world of fantasy, so I put a gnome on top of one to form this whimsical carving. Atop his mushroom, he can watch over your home.

Materials:

- A blank cut to 7¼" (184mm) high, 3¼" (83mm) wide, and 3¼" (83mm) deep
- Krylon matte finish
- Watco natural finishing wax
- Watco dark finishing wax
- Acrylic paints of choice (I use Flesh, Pale Blue, Raw Sienna, Red, Moss Green, Blue, Burnt Sienna, Black, and White by Jo Sonja and Delta Ceramcoat)

Tools:

- Carving knives, gouges, and V-tools of choice
- Band saw
- Pencil

Special Sources: *Basswood rough outs of A Gnome with a View are available for $18 plus s&h. Contact Floyd Rhadigan at 734-649-3259 or visit www.fantasycarving.com.*

The author used these products for the project. Substitute your choice of brands, tools, and materials as desired.

Front

Left

Back

Gnomes and Dwarves

Gnomes are mythological creatures appearing in tales and legends primarily of European origin. It seems the first written description or mention of gnomes is in the writings of Paracelsus of Switzerland in the 1500s.

According to legend, gnomes are small creatures with a human appearance, often described as old men. In some cases, they are disfigured, with hunched backs. Gnomes are usually reported to live underground, guarding vast treasures, and are said to move through the earth as easily as sea creatures move through water. Their underground dwellings might protect them from sunlight, which is said to turn them to stone. In Scandinavian legend, however, gnomes are forest dwellers who serve as guardians over the natural world, especially plants and animals.

In Dutch and German legends, gnomes are friendly spirits who aid humans with housework. These legends led to the creation of the first garden gnomes in Germany in the mid-1800s, as gnomes would supposedly come out to help with the gardening at night. It is from the Dutch tradition that we get the modern image of gnomes with beards and pointed hats that has become so popularized.

Right

A Gnome with a View

FRONT

LEFT

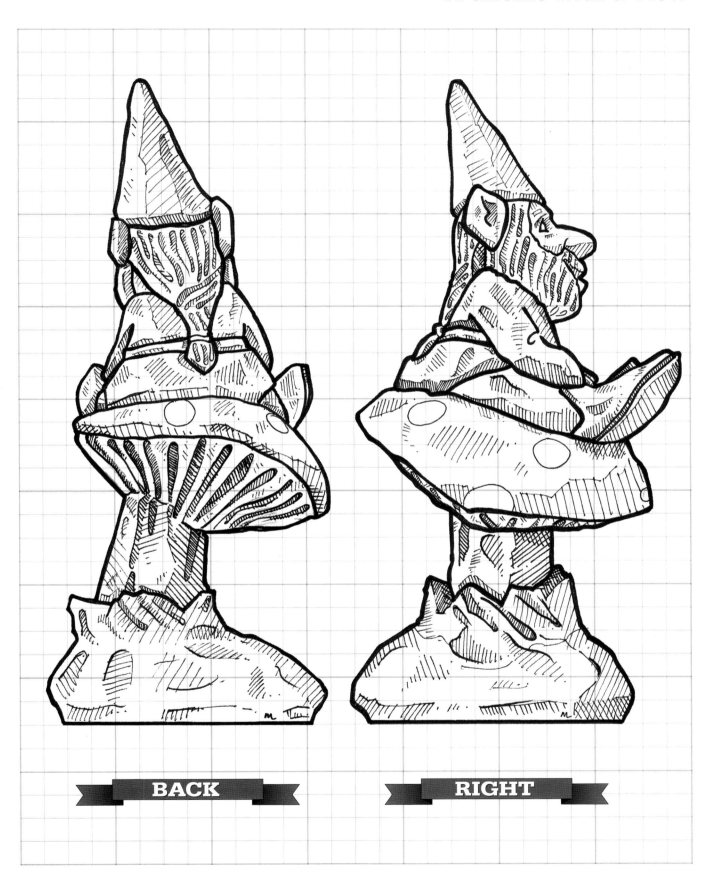

BACK

RIGHT

O'Rhadigan

Because I am of Irish descent, I thought I would carve myself an Irish gentleman. To fit the cane in his hand more easily, drill a ³⁄₁₆" (5mm) hole in the blank where the hand will be. Then, shape the hand and carve the cane to fit the hole.

Materials:

- A blank cut to 9" (229mm) high, 4¾" (121mm) wide, and 3¼" (83mm) deep
- Krylon matte finish
- Watco natural finishing wax
- Watco dark finishing wax
- Acrylic paints of choice (I use Flesh, Olive Green, Burnt Sienna, Yellow Ochre, Burnt Umber, Green, Blue, Gold, Black, and White by Jo Sonja and Delta Ceramcoat)

Tools:

- Carving knives, gouges, and V-tools of choice
- Band saw
- Pencil

Special Sources: *Basswood rough outs of O'Rhadigan are available for $25 plus s&h. Contact Floyd Rhadigan at 734-649-3259 or visit www.fantasycarving.com.*

The author used these products for the project. Substitute your choice of brands, tools, and materials as desired.

| Front | Left | Back | Right |

The Luck of the Irish?

Contrary to popular belief, having "the luck of the Irish" is not an indicator of good fortune. In fact, it's quite the opposite. This is an ironic phrase focused on the fact that, as a whole, the Irish tend to be very unlucky. As evidence, consider the conflict between English Protestant settlers and traditional Irish Catholics that arose in Ireland in the 1640s and led to Oliver Cromwell's invasion of the country in 1649. In 1845, an outbreak of potato blight destroyed almost all the potato crops across Ireland, sparking the Irish Potato Famine. Consequently, Ireland's population dropped by about one quarter, an estimated 1 million dying as a result of the famine and ineffective aid from Britain and another 1 million fleeing the country.

The advent of the twentieth century did little to bring luck back into the Irish's corner. In 1916, members of a rebel faction within Ireland attempted to lead an uprising against the British in the conflict known as the Easter Rising. The British put down the rebellion within a week, killing many of the rebels and arresting hundreds. This was followed by the Irish War of Independence (1919–1921) in which the Irish Republican Army (IRA) fought against the British for Ireland's freedom. Finally, the Anglo-Irish Treaty, signed in December 1921, established the Irish Free State separate from British rule in the south of Ireland, while several counties in northern Ireland loyal to the British were to remain a part of the United Kingdom. Despite winning the south of Ireland for themselves, some members of the IRA opposed the Anglo-Irish Treaty and sought to reignite the revolution to gain control of Northern Ireland. The result was a civil war between pro-treaty and anti-treaty factions that lasted from 1922 to 1923.

Despite all this, the Irish have proven themselves to be a strong, persistent, and enduring people. But going forward, you might want to consider just how you use the phrase "the luck of the Irish."

O'Rhadigan

Pipe Handle

FRONT

LEFT

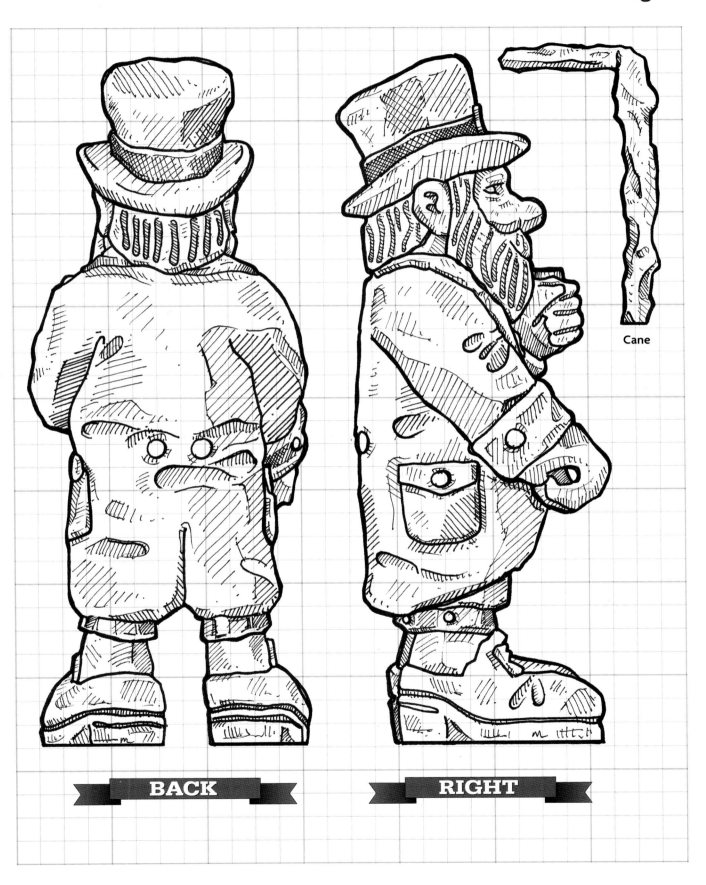

Cane

BACK

RIGHT

Orc Patrol

J. R. R. Tolkien's *The Lord of the Rings* book series inspired me to make this character. He is a guardian of the realm. As with previous carvings that had inserts, drill a ³⁄₁₆" (5mm) hole for the spear before carving the hand. Then, carve the spear shaft to fit the hole.

Materials:

- A blank cut to 6" (152mm) high, 3" (76mm) wide, and 4" (102mm) deep
- Krylon matte finish
- Watco natural finishing wax
- Watco dark finishing wax
- Acrylic paints of choice (I use Flesh, Burgundy, Burnt Umber, Burnt Sienna, Yellow, Hookers Green, Red, Gold, Black, and White by Jo Sonja and Delta Ceramcoat)

Tools:

- Carving knives, gouges, and V-tools of choice
- Band saw
- Pencil

Special Sources: *Basswood rough outs of Orc Patrol are available for $20 plus s&h. Contact Floyd Rhadigan at 734-649-3259 or visit www.fantasycarving.com.*

The author used these products for the project. Substitute your choice of brands, tools, and materials as desired.

Front

Left

Back

Right

The Origin of Orcs

Although often associated with the demon-like creatures in J. R. R. Tolkien's *The Lord of the Rings* series, the word "orc" can actually refer to sea monsters. In this case, the word is likely a derivation of *orca*, a Latin word that describes such marine life as whales and dolphins. In Old English texts, however, "orc" and other similar words are used to name demons, ogres, and monsters. For example, Grendel, the murderous creature of the epic poem *Beowulf* is referred to as *orcnéas*, which can be translated to "devil" or "monster." Tolkien's orcs fit much better with this latter description. Orcs have been adopted by many as part of fantasy games and stories and maintain a variety of appearances, powers, and magical capabilities. Almost universally, though, they are a force for evil.

Orc Patrol

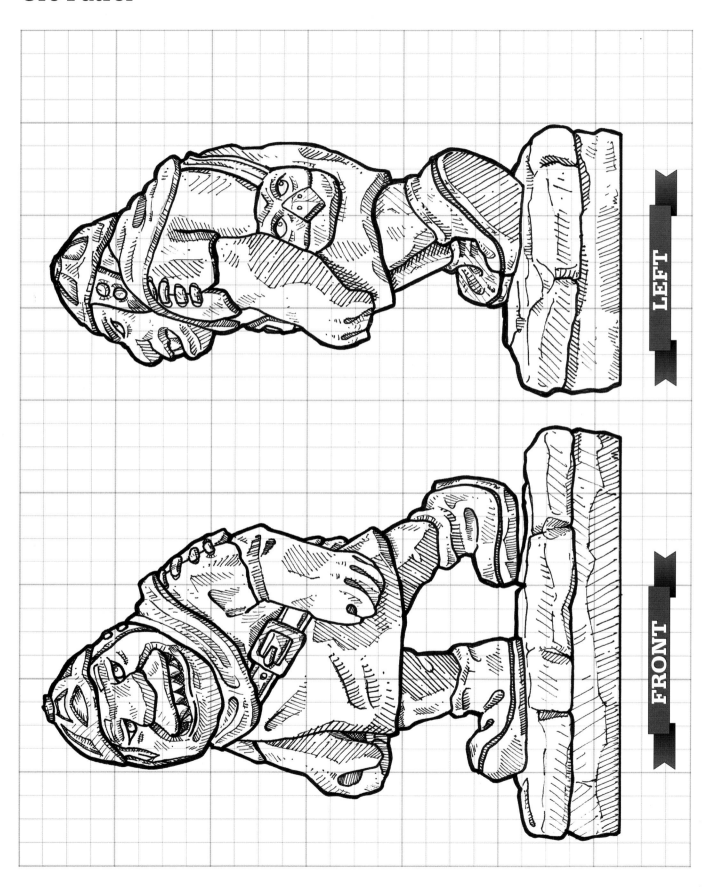

LEFT

FRONT

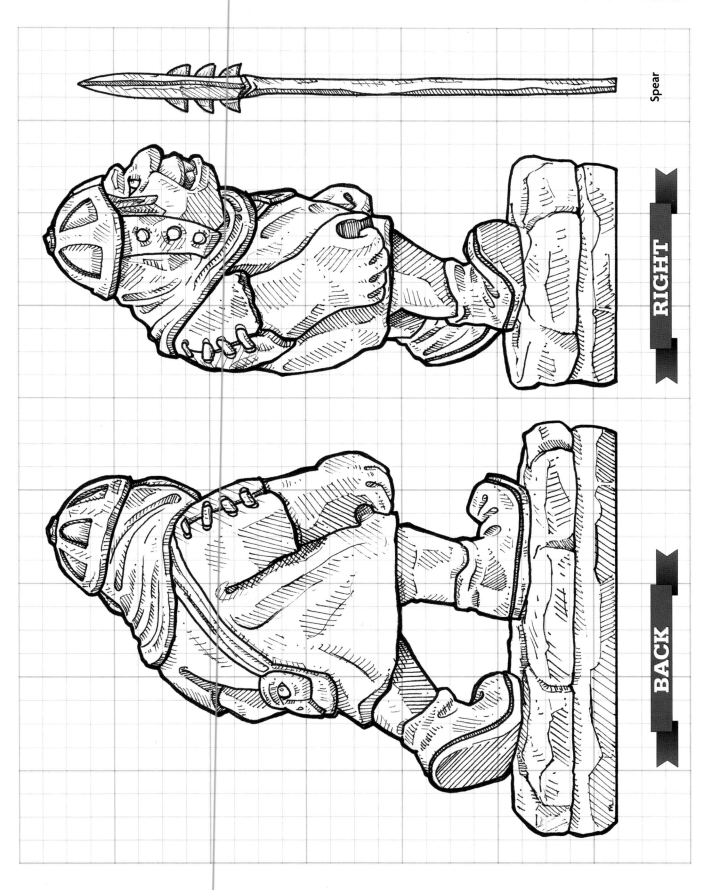

Spear

RIGHT

BACK

Nazdar the Wicked

With the help of her owl, she can cast a powerful spell. Carve the owl last to minimize your chances of breaking it. Note: Her crystal ball is just a glass marble I glued to her hand.

Materials:

- A blank cut to 8" (203mm) high, 3½" (89mm) wide, and 2¾" (70mm) deep
- Glass marble
- Krylon matte finish
- Watco natural finishing wax
- Watco dark finishing wax
- Acrylic paints of choice (I use Flesh, Yellow, Burnt Sienna, Yellow Ochre, Grey, Burgundy, Black, and White by Jo Sonja and Delta Ceramcoat)

Tools:

- Carving knives, gouges, and V-tools of choice
- Band saw
- Pencil

Special Sources: *Basswood rough outs of Nazdar the Wicked are available for $20 plus s&h. Contact Floyd Rhadigan at 734-649-3259 or visit www.fantasycarving.com.*

The author used these products for the project. Substitute your choice of brands, tools, and materials as desired.

Front

Left

Back

The 'Magic' of Crystal Balls

For centuries, reflective and/or transparent surfaces such as water, mirrors, and crystals have been used in the practice of divination. In ancient times, this might have been connected to the thought that a reflection was a devil or otherworldly figure. Certainly if you are not paying attention, an unexpected reflection can catch you off guard and elicit some kind of response. Regardless of why the tradition started, it is clear that groups such as the Druids and others claiming to be seers, sorcerers, and fortune tellers often utilized crystals as a means to see into the past or future or answer questions. Queen Elizabeth I was known to consult Dr. John Dee, a scientist noted for his use of crystal balls. While many associate crystal ball "scrying" with the appearance of images within the ball that can be interpreted as a message of some form, many who use them state that gazing into the crystal is a way of preparing oneself to receive messages by focusing and clearing the mind, much like one would do during meditation.

Right

Nazdar the Wicked

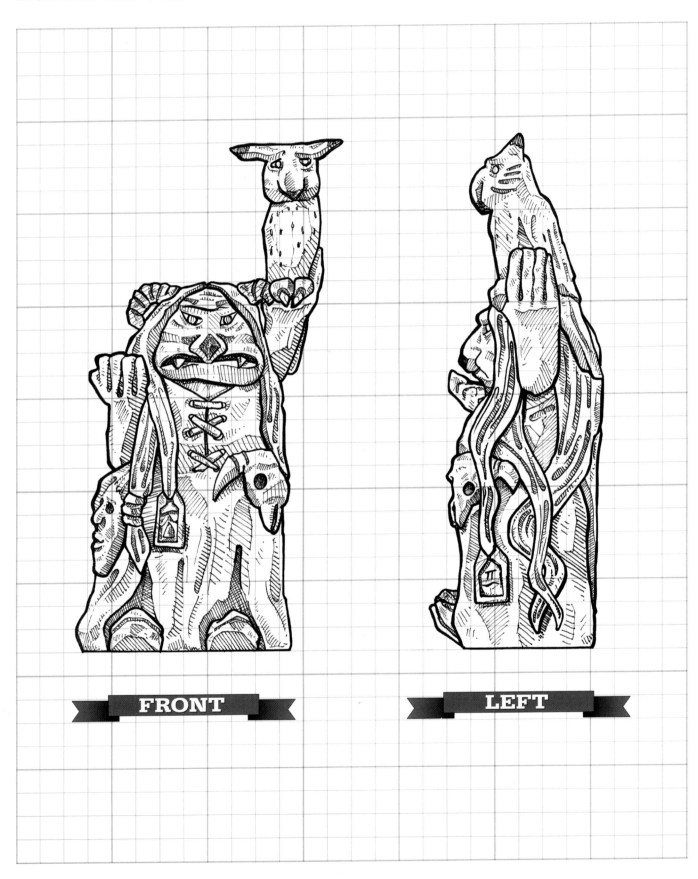

FRONT

LEFT

BACK

RIGHT

The Harvest Queen

Nothing will grow in the realm without the help of the Harvest Queen and her servant Igor. For this project, carve the Harvest Queen's hands. Then, drill a ³⁄₁₆" (5mm) hole through each hand, angling the holes away from he front of her body. Carve the sickle and pitchfork to fit the holes.

Materials:

- A blank cut to 7" (178mm) high, 2¼" (57mm) wide, and 6¼" (159mm) deep
- Krylon matte finish
- Watco natural finishing wax
- Watco dark finishing wax
- Acrylic paints of choice (I use Flesh, Grey, Burnt Sienna, Red, Burgundy, Yellow Ochre, Blue, Black, and White by Jo Sonja and Delta Ceramcoat)

Tools:

- Carvings knives, gouges, and V-tools of choice
- Band saw
- Pencil

Special Sources: *Basswood rough outs of The Harvest Queen are available for $25 plus s&h. Contact Floyd Rhadigan at 734-649-3259 or visit www.fantasycarving.com.*

The author used these products for the project. Substitute your choice of brands, tools, and materials as desired.

Front

Left

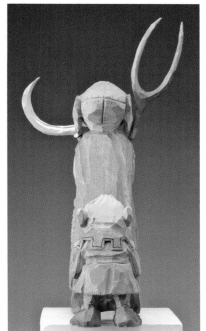

Back

Demeter: Goddess of the Harvest

Demeter is the Greek goddess of the harvest or agriculture who was responsible for the growth of crops and other plants on the earth. Demeter is also connected to the division of the year into separate seasons. There are many versions of the story of Demeter and the earth's seasons, but the basic tale is as follows.

Demeter greatly loved her daughter Persephone, but Hades, the god of the underworld, desired Persephone as his wife. Hades captured Persephone with the help of Zeus, bringing her to the underworld and making her his wife. Demeter was stricken with grief over the loss of her daughter and began to roam the earth in search of Persephone. During her search, she abandoned her duties to the earth so that the crops failed and mankind suffered. In order to persuade Demeter to return to her duties, Zeus arranged an agreement between Hades and Demeter that Persephone would be able to spend eight months of the year on the earth with her mother and the remaining four months as queen of the underworld. Demeter agreed, and during the time her daughter was with her, the earth was prosperous and able to bring forth fruit and grain. When Persephone returned to Hades, however, Demeter was so grieved that the earth remained barren during those four months.

Right

The Harvest Queen.

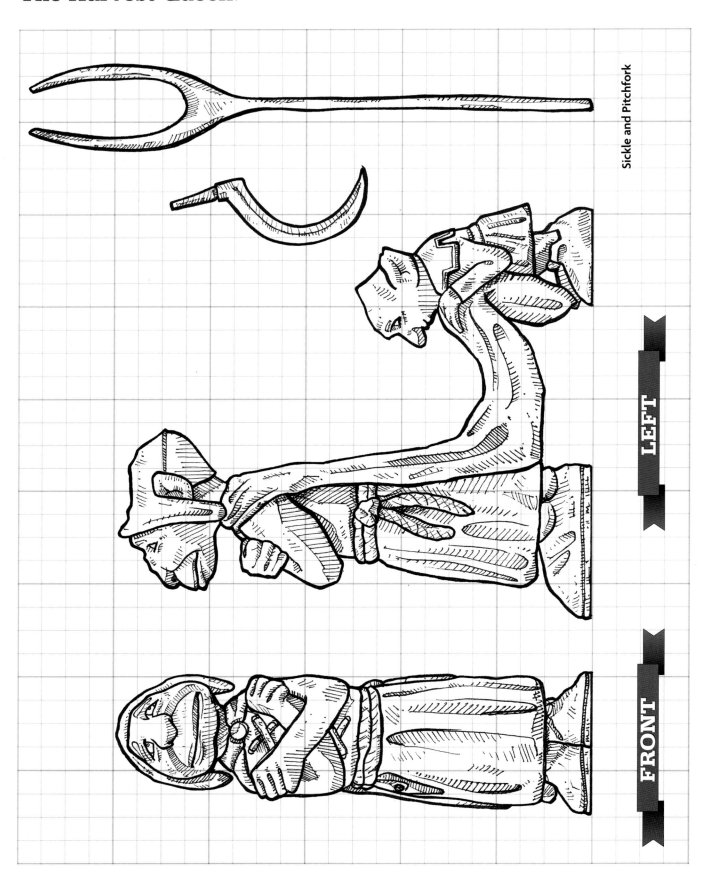

Sickle and Pitchfork

LEFT

FRONT

RIGHT

BACK

Bonus Patterns

In this section, you will find even more characters from my world of fantasy carvings. You can make them using the same tools you used to carve the previous projects. Add some color using the acrylic paints of your choice.

Brunhilde

This Brunhilde has the same blue eyes as her valkyrie namesake and will gladly offer a toothpick to all. It helps to drill the hole for the toothpicks in the blank before you begin any carving. Make the hole ¾" (19mm) in diameter and 1½" (38mm) deep.

Basswood rough outs of Brunhilde are available for $12 plus s&h. Contact Floyd Rhadigan at 734-649-3259 or visit www.fantasycarving.com.

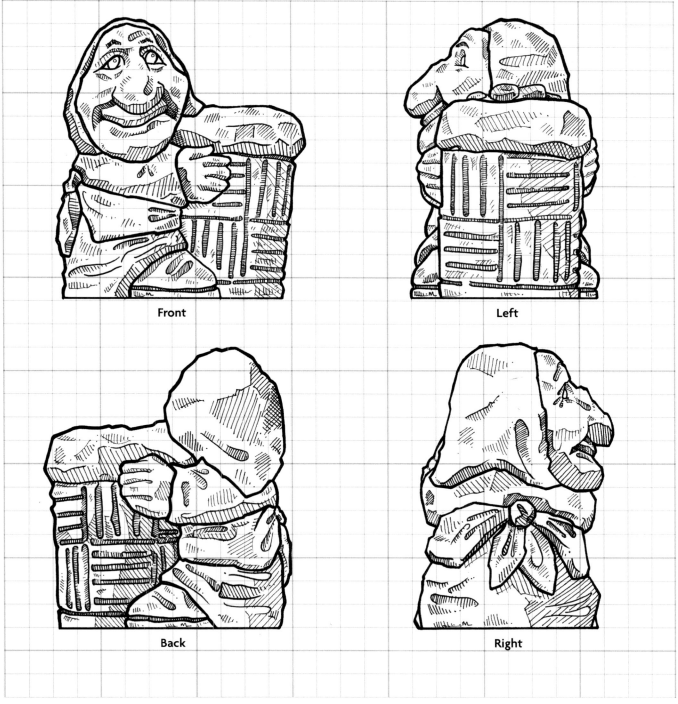

Front

Left

Back

Right

O'Ryan

O'Ryan lives up on your shelf, pondering his next mischievous deed. You might notice he has a similar feel to the Cortney and Nicole the Pixie carvings (pages 38 and 42). He was made for my son, while the other two shelf carvings were made for my two daughters.

Basswood rough outs of O'Ryan are available for $18 plus s&h. Contact Floyd Rhadigan at 734-649-3259 or visit www.fantasycarving.com.

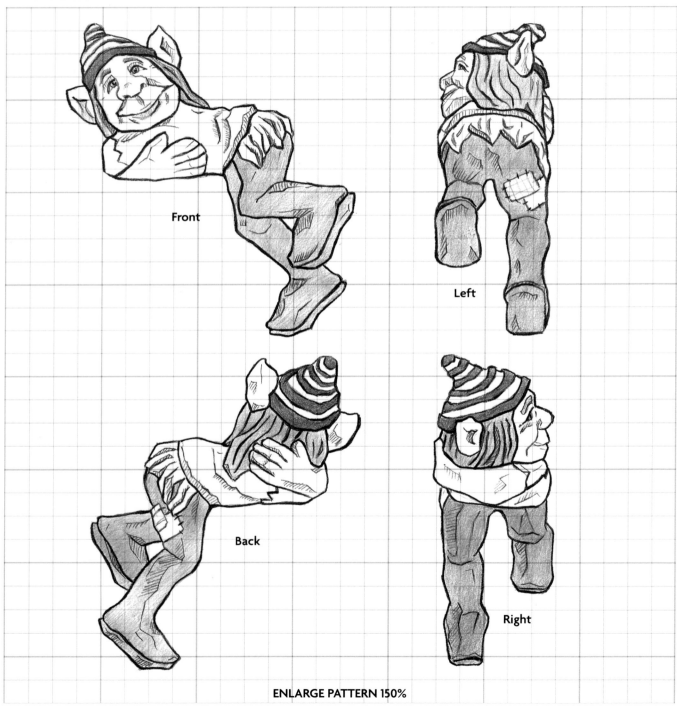

Front

Left

Back

Right

ENLARGE PATTERN 150%

The Raven Keeper

The raven is a significant symbol in many cultures. I thought the one I carved should have company, so I made the Raven Keeper. To make fitting the Raven Keeper's perch in his hand easier, drill a ³⁄₁₆" (5mm) hole in the area of the blank that will form the hand. Then, shape the hand and carve the perch shaft to fit the hole.

Basswood rough outs of The Raven Keeper are available for $18 plus s&h. Contact Floyd Rhadigan at 734-649-3259 or visit www.fantasycarving.com.

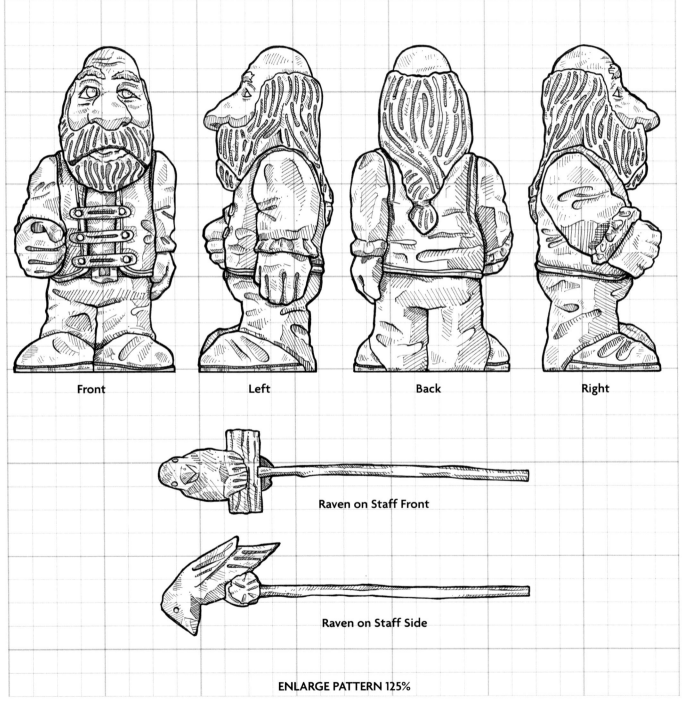

Front   Left   Back   Right

Raven on Staff Front

Raven on Staff Side

ENLARGE PATTERN 125%

The Wood Chopper

With ax in hand, the Wood Chopper is ready to work. Remember to drill a ³⁄₁₆" (5mm) hole in his hand before carving it. Then, shape the ax handle to fit the hole. I also drilled a hole in his other hand and added some twigs to represent the wood he is gathering.

Basswood rough outs of The Wood Chopper are available for $20 plus s&h. Contact Floyd Rhadigan at 734-649-3259 or visit www.fantasycarving.com.

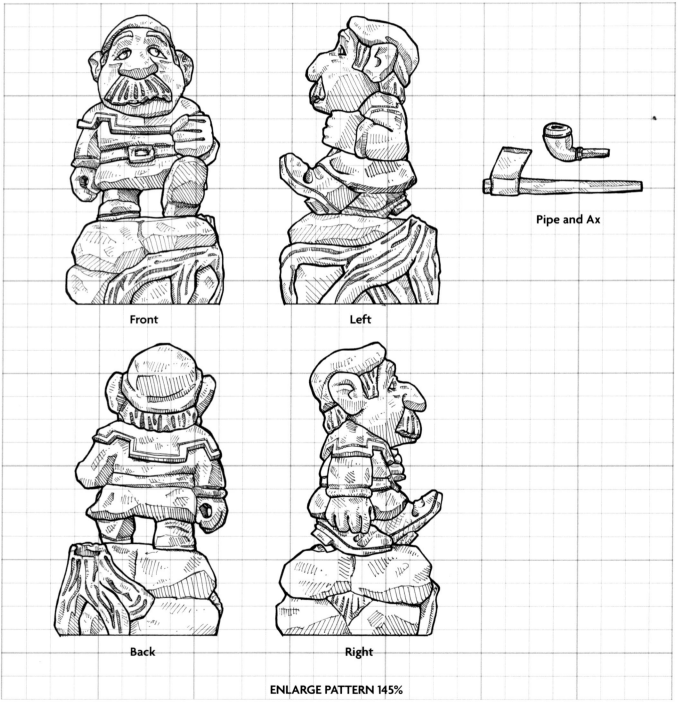

Front

Left

Pipe and Ax

Back

Right

ENLARGE PATTERN 145%

Index

ACQUISITION EDITOR: Peg Couch   **COPY EDITORS:** Paul Hambke & Heather Stauffer   **COVER & LAYOUT DESIGNER:** Jason Deller
COVER & INTERIOR PHOTOGRAPHER: Scott Kriner   **EDITOR:** Katie Weeber   **PROOFREADER:** Lynda Jo Runkle   **INDEXER:** Jay Kreider

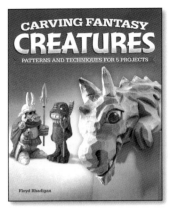
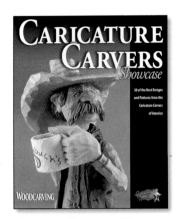
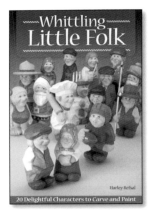

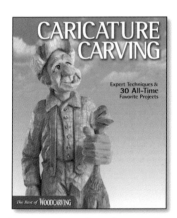
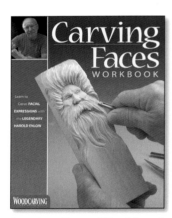